BE THE VILLAIN

SHAIK YASEEN AHMAD

ACKNOWLEDGEMENTS

For this book, there are contributions from many people, both directly and indirectly, who have inspired me, taught me, and supported me.

First and foremost, I would like to express my deepest gratitude to Rohini for her unwavering dedication and invaluable support in bringing this book to life. Her editing skills, creativity and critical thinking have been instrumental in its completion, and I am eternally grateful for her support.

I would also like to extend my heartfelt thanks to Anshika Bhatt for her insightful feedback, tireless commitment, and for reading multiple drafts with such care. Her ideas and encouragement have enriched this book immensely.

Additionally, I want to thank Noa Birens for her support even before this book began. As a poet herself, her insights were invaluable, and her encouragement meant a great deal throughout this journey.

A special thank you to Rimsha Naaz Sayeda, Parvathini Sri Anjana Chowdary, Hajna Shaik, Aparnaa M , Sareena Ismath M, and Shikha Jain for their help with proofreading and for their unwavering friendship and support.

About the Author

Shaik Yaseen Ahmad is a passionate business consultant and creative strategist who believes deeply in simplicity and making things work. Known for his unique approach to problem-solving, he loves research, strategizing, identifying pain points, and turning complex challenges into clear solutions—principles that inspired him to start his consulting business.

Since a young age, Yaseen has explored various creative pursuits, from filmmaking and photography to writing, always driven by a love of learning and growth. In college, he founded the Catalyst Club, a space dedicated to teaching the art of research and cultivating a research-driven mindset among like-minded individuals and his juniors.

In Be the Villain, Yaseen shares his personal insights on resilience, leadership, and the strength found in facing life's challenges. His journey of building businesses, consulting, and experimenting with nearly 22 projects has shaped his unique perspective. Through his work, he inspires others to focus on clarity, growth, and confidence as they navigate their own paths.

TABLE OF CONTENTS

BE THE VILLAIN

Author's Note

"The idea for this book came unexpectedly while I was writing another project. I thought I could write it over a weekend—just a couple of days and be done—but it quickly turned into something bigger. In two days, I wrote 30-40 poems. Yet, the more I wrote, the more ideas flowed. Eventually, this book consumed me, becoming the longest project I've ever worked on. No matter how much I tried to pause, I kept coming back to it.

The quote that inspired it all was one I used to tell myself as a child:
The strongest are those who fight others' demons, even when they have their own.

That led me to question: What is true strength? And who, in our world, truly embodies it? The answer, to me, was villains.

Villains have fascinated me since childhood. They possess a unique kind of strength—the kind that commands respect, ignites fear, and drives them to achieve something great. Villains aren't just evil for the sake of being evil; they are complex, intelligent, and driven individuals. They are the ones who burn with ambition to change the world and leave a legacy, the ones who never give up, even when the odds are against them.

Unlike the heroes who are often gifted with powers, villains work hard to earn their mastery. They aren't simply "bad guys"; they're thinkers, strategists, and visionaries. This book explores those kinds of villains—the ones who have struggled, grown stronger, and earned their power.

This is not a research paper or a deep dive into villain archetypes (a topic I'd like to explore someday), but my personal perspective on what a true villain is: their struggles, vulnerabilities, desires, and transformations. Villains, in many ways, represent what it means to be fully human—flawed, ambitious, and sometimes misunderstood.

This book is not just about villains; it's about inspiring you. It's about empowering you to think differently, grow stronger, and create your own path. Like the villains I write about, you too can be unique, driven, and powerful. Every villain has their own story, and so do you.

I hope this book helps you find your own strength and inspires you to keep pushing toward greatness. Thank you.

Chapter 0 - Introduction

On a sunny day,
A young naive boy, walking the streets of a kingdom,
With nothing but:
An empty pocket,
A broken heart,
A wide smile,
And his dear horse.

He sees a man,
Being tortured by the Kingsmen,
In the middle of a crowd.
The young boy filled with anger,
Rushes to help him.

"The man is punished
For not being able to pay his debt!"
Shouts one of the kingsmen

Without a second thought,
The young boy gives away his dear horse
to save the man.
The crowd disperses,
The boy left with a wide smile,
Keeps walking, undeterred.

Suddenly, he is stopped by someone,

A figure in strange clothing,
He asks the young boy,
"Your morality is your biggest weakness, boy."
The boy responds," But it also might be my true
strength."
The man laughs, a deep unsettling laugh.
"You talk like a fool. What are you seeking in the
village?"
The young boy grins,
"I'm here to have fun and learn."

The stranger's eyes flicker, fierce and fiery.
'Meet me in the forest tonight," the man says.
Before disappearing.

The boy was taken aback, his heart a whirlwind of
uncertainty,
As he wanders the new city.
He couldn't help but shake the memory of the man's
eyes—
So full of fire, so full of something unknown.

He has heard rumors circulating the town,
About a man,
He heard a merchant say,
"The master of villains has entered the kingdom,

The teacher of the seven greatest villains of the world."
world."
Another fisherman saying
"The lord of the demons
One who rules and owns them,
Breathes in our midst."
A goldsmith saying
"The most ruthless yet loving monster is wandering these streets.
A monster that devours everything that goes against."

The boy can't stop wondering if the man he met
Could the man be *him?*
His curiosity grows as the day passes.
Rumors swirl.
Some loved him, while some hated him
Some needed him, while some feared him
Some deemed him as great, and some as waste
Some talked about his ruthless conquest,
The times when he was the conqueror of the lands and seas.
Of villains and demons he once commanded.
A manipulator, a destroyer of worlds.
He devoured evil monsters of the world with his simple evil laugh

Everyone fears his presence, even the people who love
him
His ambition and desires exceed what could be
possible.

The boy can't help but wonder
Is the man in the strange clothing the one they fear?
The one some hate, but others admire,
The villain?

But his curiosity got the best of him,
And he went to the forest.
He kept waiting in the middle of the forest.
In the cold, dark forest
Surrounded by eerie sounds,
Shadows moving in the night.
He wanted to run away.
But something—
Something deeper kept him waiting.

Even in the cold winds,
Dark shadows going nearby
Sounds echoing in the forest

He kept waiting
Through the darkness,

A figure emerges, walking like a king.
With no fear,
A man in his seventies, but looking like he's forty,
He comes close.

In the darkness,
His eyes are filled with intensity
With every thud of his step,
His legs show his muscular form
Arms full of veins,
Which pulsate with strength.
A body filled with scars
And a smile on his face
A dark ominous energy radiates from him.
He is walking like the ruler of darkness,
The king of hell,
With no fear and absolute strength.

The boy, curious
His eyes wide,
With admiration.
There was no doubt now—
This is *him*.
The villain.

The boy's mind swirls with questions

Voices of the kingdom echoing in his head.
As the man steps forward,
He bombards him with questions:
"Who are you?
Where are you from?
Why did you invite me here?
What's happening?
Are the people in the city talking about *you*?

The man just relaxes himself on the ground
Leaning against a rock.
He smiles.
The boy's racing mind calms.
He pauses,
Then, with a quiet voice, he asks one final question:

"Master... Who are Villains?
I want to know more
I want to know their stories
I want to understand their thoughts".

CHAPTER 1 - WHO ARE VILLAINS

Villains walk the path less traveled,
Who dares to go alone,
Who has the strength to keep pursuing,
Who has the anger to drive them on,
Who seeks mastery in his every path,
Their power ever-growing,
And though you walk where they have gone,
The pain in the paths is lessened.
For the love of pain, they endure it all,
So others might feel none.
A burden none can share.
The weight they carry, all on themselves,
Which no one dare imagine.

The pain of the past runs through their veins.
The anger of centuries flows through their blood.
They channel it all into their work,
Crafting the most intense masterpiece
The world has ever seen.

They walk in the shadows,
Through the darkness,
To bring light to the world.
They take the hardest paths,
Bearing the weight of suffering,
So none need to bear.

They bear scars all over them, from the battles they
fought.
Each scar has a story.
With every scar, their fear starts to cease,
Preparing them to fight new battles,
Ready to bleed themselves for the sake of others.

They are neither good nor evil,
They are free.
With no desires or ambitions,
They act only from the essence of their nature—
A villain, without pretense or purpose.

Life doesn't favor them,
Society turns away,
Luck is never on their side,
But they never keep their chin down,
They refuse to fear the storm,
When the winds don't blow their way.
With a grin, they face struggle.
Looking for opportunities to grow and become stronger.

Life throws countless curveballs,
Hits them hard,
Fails and defeats them.
But every time,
They laugh,
Chest out, facing life head-on.
They ask for more,
And show who is truly in charge.

Hero's sacrifice their people,
To save the world.
The villain burns down the world,
To save his people.

They aren't noble,
They don't act noble,
They don't deceive or put on a show.
They are blunt and straightforward,
They have no facade to sell you.
What you see is what you get—
Genuine, though not always warm.

They constantly await for battles greater than the last,
Driven to become stronger.
Challenges are their home
Without challenges, they feel restless,
When a challenge arises,
They smile and steady themselves like a charging bull,
Ready to strike in the next fight.

They have no patience for false heroes,
Those who wear a mask and play make-believe.
They prefer the company of those who seem genuine,
Even if they are villains.
They value authenticity over facade
And aim to build a rawer, truer connection with those
who are real.

Villains are genuine,
Nothing to lie about,
Nothing to gain from you,
And nothing to prove to you.
They don't mind being hated on or mocked at.
They stand firm,
Aware of who they are.

They are polarizing,
Some hate them,
While others are drawn to them— not with love,
But with a strong, undeniable pull.

They were once failures,
They were once looked down upon.
But with each setback,
They rose again,
Each failure made them stronger,
Strengthening their winds with every challenge.
In no time, they built storms of their own,
Sweeping those away who dared to look down upon
them.
And suddenly, no one could ignore their presence.

They are unafraid to speak the truth,
Facing the greedy enemies who lie.
Without their courage, the truth will die,
And greedy liars they will ply

Winning their hearts is difficult,
They care deeply for the world and the universe,
But are hesitant to accept love in return.
Yet if you manage to love them,
You are embracing the entire world with your love—
not just them.

A villain is cunning, sharp and wise,
Never gets in fights he can't win for the pride,
He runs away like a coward, avoids the fight.
But as he waits, he silently grows,
And when he enters the fight, he strikes with might,
Like a forest fire, fast and bright.

They don't claim to know it all,
Neither are they blinded by their egos.
Humbled by the lessons they find,
Always seeking to expand their mind.
They are never old,
Always seeking new things to learn.
True villains are smart, it's clear to see,
Always growing, endlessly.

The man at the top is often the loneliest,
Much like villains who are frequently alone.
Both stand apart, isolated by their positions and
choices.

A villain has new chapters in every phase

With each phase, they are different

They evolve

Becoming stronger and trying new challenges are their

hobbies

They are slaves to no one,
Not controlled by anyone's thoughts,
Not even their doubts or desires.
They live freely, guided by their own will,
Answerable only to themselves.

A villain needs no gang and no loyal followers.
People are drawn to them,
Not by force, but by their strength and power.
Everyone wants to rest under the shade of a great tree,
Everyone wants to associate with the strong.

They are troublemakers and problem solvers,
Despised by society,
But cherished by those who truly know them.

Love.
They love their friends.
But to their friends, they're the enemy.
Reaching the top brings isolation,
Yet, the villain never stops loving.
Because deep down, that's all they know—
To love, even when it isn't returned.

They don't seek enemies,
But greedy heroes want to be their enemies.
They dwell in peace,
But violence surrounds them.

They are always at peace
For countless battles have made them fearless.
The numerous scars have turned them tough,
And carrying the burden of their kin,
Has made them indestructible.

Villains are the god of trickery
Villains are the gods of naughtiness
Villains are the gods of cunningness
Villains are the gods of shrewdness
Villains are the gods of playfulness
They are the gods of fascination

They never speak of themselves,
And praise has no effect on them.
Whether the world mocks or applauds,
It's all the same to them.
Because they are anchored in self-awareness—
They know exactly who they are.

They are soft
Vulnerable
Humble
Gentle
But no one knows it
For the greedy heroes, they are the devils of hell

Sharing comes naturally to them,
Even when they have nothing to give.
Caring is their instinct,
Even they are worn and tired.
Moving forward is their way,
Even they stumble and fall.

They are unable to see others in pain,
So they silently pray,
"Let all the world's pain be mine to carry."
And through this burden,
They become the strongest of all.

Heroes wage wars
To protect their beliefs, grudges and pride.
Villains are pulled into battle,
To protect the world.

True Villains are creators,
Builders who get things done.
They drive the world forward,
To create wealth and opportunity.
Their passion fuels up the world,
Their madness shapes new directions.
They pave the way for the future.

True strength of the villain,
Doesn't lie in his body,
Nor in his kin,
Nor in his wealth,
Their thought process is their biggest strength.

They work out,
They exercise
They want to find the highest potential of their body
and mind
Their goal is to reach the heights

They are charming,
Manipulative,
Liars, and jerks.
But they are, Who they are.
And they embrace it.
Everything they do,
Is for the sake of their near and dear ones,
And, in the end, for the world.

They embody narcissism and ego,
They embrace it, using it as fuel to grow.
Instead of suppressing these traits,
They harness them to evolve—
And eventually, rise beyond them.

They are self-aware,
Fully knowing their weaknesses,
The shadows that linger within,
Their moments of hypocrisy,
And their narcissism,
Their understanding drives their growth,
Pushing them to confront and overcome.

They don't judge others;
They have no time for gossip and judgment.
Their focus lies inward,
On their own journey,
Leaving no room for the noise of others.

Just as diamonds are made under immense pressure,
Villains are shaped by
The toughest trials,
Traumatic experiences,
And days of suffocating struggle.

I will achieve my dream
Even if it means facing every demon,
Enduring all the pain,
Confronting the darkness,
And embracing every failure.
It doesn't matter what stands in my way—
I will achieve my dream,
I will rise above it all,
And I will achieve my dream.

No matter how hard life tries to break me,

I will never surrender.

One day, I'll make life regret ever thinking i'd give in

I'll turn its tests in triumphs,
And make it look foolish for trying to defeat me.

The people pray for a life without problems.
And when problems arise, they kneel down and cry,
They complain and search for a way out.
But the villain greets problems with a wicked grin,
Looking life in the eye and saying "Is that all you got'?
Life's brutal attacks mean nothing to him,
His smile never fades.
He doesn't flinch, He challenges life,
Daring it to hit harder.

Chapter 2 - Strength

The boy looked up,
"Master, I would love to hear a story of one of your
students."
The master nodded,
"I will tell you about Tamish.
A man who faced great suffering and suffocation,
And still chose strength."

"He was betrayed
Cast aside,
Mocked and laughed at."

"Yet through it all,
He rose up.
Stronger than ever
Refusing to break."

The boy's eyes lit up and filled with admiration.
He leaned in,
And the master began the story,
The tale of Tamish—

In the far lands,
Within a kingdom ruled by greed,
A rebel—defiant against the corrupt kings—
Has been captured.

In the courtroom,
He was punished,
Beaten, attacked,
Slapped by the very people he once loved.
Blood streamed through his scars,
His eyes grew heavy,
On the brink of closing.

He was asked to bow before everyone—
All the kings, ministers and people,
Had a grin on their face,
As they saw him suffer.
Then, discarding him like trash,
They threw him into the wastelands.

But he stood up,
His body broken,
Yet, determined by his mind,
To be the *strongest.*

The body is exhausted,
And every step feels like a thousand,
Like walking on a land full of thorns.
The body ready to give up,
Eyes filled with exhaustion,
Feets which won't stop trembling,
The back begged for mercy.
But the mind is determined,
Pushing to reach it's final destination.
And so, he keeps moving forward.

Day by day
Learning, growing,
Challenging himself,
Waiting with patience.

Years passed,
And he became a king of another nation,
And the day came,
When he returned,
To wreck the liars and greedy kings.
Who had wronged him.

And they all had to bow down to their new king,
The same rebel they had once tried to crush.

As a rebel, he had always been driven by anger—
He was unable to stop himself,
When he saw something wrong.
He fought bigger enemies,
Faced so-called heroes,
Who wore masks of righteousness,
But were secretly destroying the public.

He decided to fight them all,
Yet once again,
He was outnumbered.

But yet again, he lost.
Back to being chained and caged,
The world moved forward,
While the villain remained trapped,
In a dark, suffocating room.

Everyday, from morning till night,
He pulled at those chains relentlessly,
Trying to break from the shackles,
But it's stronger than mountains.
His foes celebrated,
Living in luxury,
While all he thought of was breaking free.

He keeps pulling with all his might.
Days pass by,
His strength and resilience grew,
His anger keeps filling him up.
His eyes opened with intensity every morning,
Somedays were tougher than others,
Pain surrounds his body,
Suffocation makes it harder,

Every second felt like a year,
Every breath had the weight of a mountain.
He shouted in pain and for his dream to be freed,
The roar which echoed throughout the room,
Getting louder, and louder.

But he never stopped pulling.
For his dream of freedom,
The only thing that kept him alive.

Days turned into weeks,
And though he saw little progress,
He didn't stop.
Kept trying new methods,
Experimenting,
Every ounce of energy spent on his goal.

Then one day,
He heard it—
The sound of cracking.
He looked up
A wicked laugh escaped his lips.
It ignited him,
He doesn't stop pulling.

And finally,
The chains on his legs snapped.
Laughing like a maniac,
Filled with a dark sense of triumph.
Waiting to break free,
He kicked open the door,
Stretched his worn body,
And the world looked upon him—
A man with a strong, muscular frame,
An evil smile,
Anger that could tear through anything.

But above all,
He possessed an unbreakable mindset.

All the suffering,
The suffocation,
The broken bones and pain,

Has made him into a warrior like no other
The anger stored within him,
The betrayal of loved ones,
Had fueled his strength.

He used every bit of that rage,
To become the greatest warrior.
To master his work to perfection,
And unleash chaos upon the world.

No one dared to speak his name,
No warrior wished to meet his wrath,
His body,
Covered in countless scars,
Bore witness to his journey—
From a rebel to the most feared being in the world.

Villains use every experience as their fuel,
Good or bad

Just as diamonds are made under immense pressure,
Villains are shaped by
The toughest trials,
Traumatic experiences,
And days of suffocating struggle.

The people pray for a life without problems.
And when problems arise, they kneel down and cry,
They complain and search for a way out.
But the villain greets problems with a wicked grin,
Looking life in the eye and saying "Is that all you got'?
Life's brutal attacks mean nothing to him,
His smile never fades.
He doesn't flinch, He challenges life,
Daring it to hit harder.

A villain was once exploited—
Not for his wickedness, but for his kindness and
naiveness.
He did good for everyone, always helpful,
But the world used him, took advantage of his heart.
He was kind, but blind to his power.
Until one day, he saw it.
He became the villain,
Not evil, just no longer a fool.

They have endured depression,
Insomnia,
Loneliness—
All the world's worst diseases.
Nights spent praying and suffering just to fall asleep,
Days in pain and hoping to just pass through.
Evenings in solitude, longing for companionship.
Nothing ever went their way.
They have been through hell,
But they still found a way out.
Never giving up,
Pushing forwards to achieve,
To be free,
To become the strongest.

A villain is not someone who never falls,
But someone who refuses to accept defeat.
He rises again and again
Like an undying serpent, relentless and unyielding.

The world told him to surrender,
 he remained silent.
He doesn't need many words,
His actions speak louder than their demands.

Your ambition makes you strong.
Your pain makes you strong.
Your suffering makes you strong.
Your bad experiences make you strong.
Your love makes you strong.
Your sharing makes you strong.
The greater your ambition is,
The bigger your pain and suffering—
And the stronger you become.
Aim high, for the higher you aim
The stronger you will grow.

"Why do people hate you?" he asked.
"People hate the truth,"
They cling to their own beliefs
And only cherish what aligns with them.
And I for one question those beliefs,
Seek the truth, and speak it.
The moment you speak the truth,
Be ready to make enemies.

"Master, but is speaking the truth necessary?" he asked.

"Without truth, liars thrive,
The greedy heroes get worshipped,
Causing more harm to the world.
Truth is the only force which holds them back," the Master replied.

"Doesn't it bother you? To be hated?" he asked

"It would only bother me if everyone loved me," he replied.

"Then I'd just be a pleaser.

Lacking any real character.

With true character,

Some will hate you,

And some will love you."

The boy asked thoughtfully,
"Master, but are struggles necessary?
There are many successful people who haven't faced struggle.
How does going through help us?"
The master laughs,
"Struggle, my child, is what gives someone the strength to truly hold their place in the world."
He paused, looking at the boy with a smile.
"Let me share with you one conversation i overheard
Between Tamish and the son of a wealthy king."

A son of a wealthy, respected hero
Approaches the young villain,
Jealousy, arrogance, and greed fueling his words.
The son says,
"You are nothing. No one.
Don't you dare challenge me.
You will lose. You don't know how powerful I am,
What I am capable of.
Back off."
The young villain laughs loudly.
And says,
O my dear hero!
You were raised in luxury,
You got everything handed to you the moment you
were born.
You were raised in comfort, without a care.
Girls flocked to you, not because of who you are,
But because of your father's name.
You were surrounded by respect,
Support and privilege.
And me?
I had no one.
People insulted me, laughed at me.
I had no support, no respect.
I grew up in mud,

Learning to survive in it.
I woke up to ruthless days.
With struggle and pain all over.
Everyday I wished to be successful and failed.
I was broken by the ones i loved,
Scared and alone—
Yet I moved forward.
These scars?
They're from my own battles,
Fought with my own strength and will.
Where i am today is because of who i am,
Not because of my father.
Don't let your arrogance blind you,
Son of a Hero.
Frustrated, The son lashes out,
"I'll tell my dad! He'll take care of you
He is a superstar and you? You're nothing."
The villain laughs again,
"Go ahead, tell you father, your uncle,
Even your grandfather.
None of them can do a thing."

The boy laughs, he asks the master,
"Master Tamish had a lot of anger,
And do you think anger is good?
People deem it as bad."
Master replies,
Anger is a necessity , let me share another story of a
warrior, Kshipa.
And how she used her anger to mastery and greatness.

CHAPTER 3 - ANGER

Story of Kshipa

In a vast kingdom,
Lived a princess with no parents.
Looked after by her brother,
The ruler of the kingdom.

She was known for her empathy,
Her compassion,
Her elegance—
The most graceful woman in the kingdom.

Her brother, a master of swords,
Taught her the art of daggers.
She learned quickly,
As if born for it.

One fateful night,
A ruthless king,
Who owned a kingdom,
Thrice the size of theirs,
Attacked without warning, without ethics.

In the war that followed,
Her brother was badly injured,
Yet rescued by his generals in the war.

The ruthless king took her kingdom
Took away her dignity and shamed her,
Along with many innocent females.

Despite her wounds,
She secretly took care of her brother.
And all the while,
She honed her skills with the swords.
Her eyes were fierce,
She was consumed by a fire that grew each day.
She slashed daggers,
With the intensity of the fiercest waters.

One day, the ruthless king found her brother.
As she stood before him and his small army,
Her blood boiled.
Without hesitation,
She ran towards them,
And in one swift motion,
She slashed the throat of the nearest man.
The king, having had enough,
He ordered her death,
And he slashed everyone who came near.
Though she was beaten and injured,
Every time she rose again,

With more power and rage,
And didn't let anyone touch her brother

One by one, she obliterated the king's men.
Then, with unstoppable force,
She dragged the ruthless king
Into the streets of the kingdom.

Covered in blood,
She slashed everyone who went against her.

All the women of the land,
Awe-struck by her ferocity,
They started beating drums,
Blowing trumpets,
Dancing and cheering for her.
While she is covered with blood
Vengeance consumed her.

The rest of the women inspired
Joined her in the fight.
The princess dragged the king,
To the center of the city.
In front of everyone,
She slashed his throat,
With a roar even the lions would fear.

She kept roaring and looking for more enemies to kill,
But then.
She saw her brother,
Walking towards her.
In that moment, she came to her human form,
And looked around her,
Taking a breath.
And finally, she stood still.

The kingdom was hers once again.
And now the world knew her—
Not just as the compassionate and elegant princess,
But as the most fierce women of all.

She manages the wealth and growth of the kingdom,
While maintaining empathy and femininity
She was once known for.

Her anger had not only avenged her,
But also sparked a revolution,
Built a new world—
A kingdom built on truth,
Where justice and honesty prevailed.
Her anger,
The most powerful emotion,
Was what gave rise to this new age of prosperity.

Anger is the purest emotion.

It's the most powerful force within us.

The more anger you carry, the more energy you possess.

If you learn to channel that anger,

They can create extraordinary things.

Never suppress your anger,

Increase it

Channelise it

Your anger, when controlled, becomes your superpower.

A lot of anger fuels great desires.

You need a lot of anger to get things done.

Anger is your fuel,

Anger can impel you to change the world,

To write powerful books,

Or create masterpieces,

It's the feeling of powerlessness that sparks great desires.

Jealousy isn't wrong—

Until it's motivating you,

Your rivals?

They are your biggest inspiration.

If someone tries to crush them or walk over them,
They plow their way through all of them.

To the world, They seem patient,
Never showing their anger.
But inside, they burn with a short temper.
They bottle up their anger,
Channeling it with purpose—
To achieve mastery,
To create masterpieces
And fight for others.

The masses stay silent when wrongs are done,
Afraid to raise their voice,
Prefer safety over confrontation.
But the villains won't back down from raising their
voices.
They can't stand by when evil prevails.
They will fight for what's right,
No matter the cost.

Student says, but master don't you think anger causes
violence
And isn't violence bad
Violence can be just when faced with wrong,
And peace can be misplaced in the face of injustice.
Learn the art of violence,
But don't let it consume you—
Instead, wield it with purpose.
Stand firm with your beliefs,
Always fight for what's right
For justice,
For everyone who suffers under the weight of
wrongdoing.

Anger without purpose is wrong,
Anger to harm others is wrong,
But anger to protect,
For justice,
Is right.

A person who is always angry,

Irritated at all times,

Is not shown respect.

Their voice becomes a nuisance.

But when anger is shown with purpose,

In moments that truly matter,

Everyone understands the meaning.

So only show anger when there is a meaning to it,

And that's how you command respect and power.

If someone abuses you,
Hit them—not with just fists,
But with resolve and strength.
Don't let them win,
You are the villain

Every battle is won first in your mind,
And only then in reality.
Every success is achieved in your thoughts,
And only then does it manifest in life.
Every pain is conquered mentally.
And only then can you overcome it in the world.
Villains have the anger to break a mountain.

Villains always yearn for peace,
Dreaming of doing what's right.
But only when greedy, arrogant heroes go astray,
Villains reveal their most violent side.

Not just their anger, their patience too is their super power just like

A tiger may hunt 20 times and succeed only once,
Yet it remains the most feared animal in the jungle.
Not because of wild rage or showmanship,
But because of its patience.
It's fierce, watchful eyes scanning the surroundings
Are the most dangerous sight any animal can witness.

The end goal is peace,
But if someone seeks war,
And you are unable to stop them,
Then prepare yourself for battle.

If someone tries to attack,

Ignore them and keep moving forward.

And if they expect an apology,

Offer it—even if it's not your mistake.

Don't let anger consume you;

Avoid unnecessary conflicts.

But if they persist,

And it becomes clear they won't stop,

Then prepare to win the war before it even begins.

Don't misinterpret my words of war and fight.
As a call for physical battles.
Most words are fought with words
And most victories are won through psychological
warfare.
Don't be foolish and rush into physical conflict.
Instead, use the tools at your disposal:
Compromise, blackmail, desire, punishment—
All without crossing the lines of legality and morality.
Think long-term.
Never do anything that will harm your future.
Be smart
Strategize,
And aim to win the war in mind.

If they resort physical force,
Counter with psychological strength.
Every person has a weakness—
Find it, use it to your advantage.

Even if the strongest attacks,
Don't let fear take hold.
Fear only breeds more fear,
Leading to anxiety and clouded judgment.
Instead, think logically.
Stay calm. Assess the situation.
And figure out their weakness.
Every opponent, no matter how powerful,
Has a vulnerability.

Every battle is won first in your mind,

And only then in reality.

Every success is achieved in your thoughts,

And only then does it manifest in life.

Every pain is conquered mentally.

And only then can you overcome it in the world.

If you want to win the battle of the mind,
Shift your focus from your opponent and your fear.
Don't overthink or overvalue them.
Focus on yourself—on your next moves.
Predict only their next step,
Stay calm, stay cool.
And look for their weakness.

Catch their weakness
And pull it on quietly.
Be stealthy—
There's no need to show off.
One well-placed strike is all it takes.
Once they feel the blow,
They will be damaged,
And that's enough to win.

Never take unnecessary risks in life—
they can damage you.
Instead, Always rely on your mind and careful
calculations.
Use strategies to make the most riskiest situations.
Into ones with little or no risks.
Your strategies are your lifelines,
Your safeguard.
Without a clear strategy,
Without a well-thought-out, visible outcome
Never take a leap.

Sometimes, life's biggest wars are with those closest to us.
We can't harm them, yet they often hurt us—
Knowingly or unknowingly.
In such moments, you have to fight,
Not with fists, but with your words and will.
Speak up until the issue is resolved.
Sometimes, you'll need to talk softly,
With charm and patience to get things done.
And at times, you need to raise your voice
To show that it's hurting.
But fighting is essential,
because without standing your ground,
there can be no true peace.

Don't always rush to fight.
If the issue is small,
Just stay calm and keep moving.
Save your energy for battles that truly matter.
The greatest fighters are those who know when to
fight.

The master continued,
"True masters Are those who learn to wield their
anger with intelligence.
When anger is tempered with wisdom,
That's when mastery is achieved."

The boy's eyes lit up,
"Master, is there someone who truly embodies this
balance.?

The master smiled knowingly,
"Yes, there is.
Let me share with you the story of Dhana—
One of the greatest masters of his craft."

CHAPTER 4 - MASTERY

Dhana,
A boy from a very small town,
Born into a family of farmers,
Had a dream:
To become the Greatest Archer in the world.

He practiced relentlessly,
Even though he was terrible at first.
Even when everyone laughed,
He never stopped.

Every day he read old books,
Sneaking off to competitions to observe,
Learning from a master in secret.
He never gave up.

After years of relentless persistence,
He became the greatest archer.

A king heard of him,
And summoned him to his court,
He asked him to shoot the fastest eagle,
And the most unpredictable squirrel.
What's so hard for most archers
Was child's play for him.

A man noticed him carefully while he shot,
His eyes full of fierceness,
A grin on his face,
A body balanced and elegant.

With every shot,
That archery became a form of art,
A dance of fire.
If he sets his eyes on a target,
He wouldn't remove them,
Even with the object moving.

He was cheered by the crowd for his performance.
He became a legend across many kingdoms,
 Known as the most talented archer in the world.

He was also appointed as the general,
Leading his kingdom in wars,
Where he outperformed everyone—
Until one fateful war,
Where he lost his right arm.

Despair consumed him.
He lost what he had trained for his entire life.
He was cast away, seen as useless.

He returned to his humble home,
With no will to live.
Every time he looked at someone with a bow,
Tears filled his eyes.

One day, he met a master,
An archer so precise,
That it took away his breath.
When he went closer,
The master pointed the bow at him,
And to his astonishment,
The master was blind,
In that moment,
A spark ignited within him—
A new hope,
A second chance at life.

And he shouted to sky
O life I challenge you to make my life as hard as you
can.
O the greatest gods, I challenge you to try your best to
stop me from reaching my goal.
No matter how much ever you try,
I won't give up.
You can't stop me.
I will come back stronger.

I will cross every obstacle,
And I am going to win."

He shouted,
'I will win!
His voice grew louder.
The clouds seemed to tremble in fear.
"I will achieve my dream!"

He requested the master to guide him
To teach him.
And the master agreed,
The master handed him an axe instead,
Asking him to hit a tree with his left arm,

He missed by a long shot.
But the master said he would teach further
When he could hit the tree.

Using his old discipline,
His principles,
His focus,
And relentless persistence ,
He trained.
Not only did he learn to hit the tree,
He learned to hit moving objects with an axe.

He became as elegant as before.

The master patted him and said;
"If you focus on what you've lost,
You will never move forward.
If you focus on what you have,
You will start.
And if you focus on what you've gained,
You will become unstoppable.
Don't dwell on what you lost,
Don't pity yourself for what you don't have,
Get up and keep moving forward.
Never settle for less
Always keep your head above and aim for the stars
Even if all you have left is your heart."

The master left,
But his words stayed,

The archer became even better.
The kings praised him once more.
The people cheered,
Tales were written after him.

He has helped countless lives,

Defeated thugs,
He became more dangerous than ever before.
His smile was larger than ever.
His story has inspired thousands.

But once again,
He faced hardship
Thugs captured him,
And paralysed his left arm.

He waited for days,
Hoping for a miracle,
But nothing changed,
He was again left with his broken arm.

He laughed,
And shouted:
"Is that all you got life?"

He never stopped his journey.
He became a king.
He became the fastest runner,
The greatest swimmer.

With only his two legs,
He could defeat anyone in a fight.

With his feet and mouth,
 He even became the greatest archer once again.
And his smile is now as wide as,
Never-ending Sky
.And he is in the most dangerous form.

Even if the world labels them with disabilities,
Villains know the truth:
They possess no such limitations.
Villains don't have any disability
The real disability lies within the mind,

Clouded by doubts and fears.
But villains, they conquer that mind,
Transforming weakness into strength.
Their greatest ability?
An unyielding steel mind,
Forged in the fires of adversity.

They prove others wrong,
They prove themselves wrong,
Everyday, They wage war within.
Pushing their limits,
Questioning their own beliefs.
They don't just seek to prove others wrong—
They seek to prove themselves wrong.
With every question and every action,
They break their boundaries
And grow beyond them.

They might stand defeated,
But they never truly lose,
They might stumble,
But never grow weak.
They might feel fear,
But their courage never fades.

They are not afraid of being hated or judged,
But they fear one thing which is:
Not trying,
Not giving their all,
Not proving their worth.

They rise each day to give their best,
Pushing themselves to do the greatest work of their
lives.
Even when frustration and stress hit,
They keep going,
Driven by the desire to excel.
No matter the struggle,
They rise again to do the best work of their life.

The hardest battles create the strongest warriors.

When we face struggles, I believe it's life's way of preparing us,

Strengthening us for a greater purpose in life.

To try to make the world better place,

So when struggles come my way, I prepare to learn and grow.

It frustrates me at sometimes, even irritates me,

But deep down, I know these challenges will make me stronger,

They will make me better.

Struggles shapes our resilience,

So we can fulfill a higher purpose in life.

Your ambition makes you strong.
Your pain makes you strong.
Your suffering makes you strong.
Your bad experiences makes you strong.
Your love makes you strong.
Your sharing makes you strong.
The greater your ambition is,
The bigger your pain and suffering—
And the stronger you become.
Aim high, for the higher you aim
The stronger you will grow.

Villains are restlessly persistent.
Persistence is their superpower.
That's how they conquer the strongest,
That's how they rise to the top.
Through failures, or in successes,
Even in pain, or joy,
Even in the worst conditions or best,
They never waver from their path.
Determined to achieve their goals,
Restless in their pursuit,
Turning obstacles into stepping stones.

They reinvent themselves as often as necessary,
Destroying their weaker selves.
To rise again, stronger and more resilient,
Each transformation is a rebirth,
A chance to shed the past
And embrace new strength.

Everything fuels a villain's motivation—
Jealousy, insults, failure and even success.
No matter what life throws at them,
They turn it into energy to push forward.
For them, every experience is a spark to grow stronger.

"Master, Are the Villains Masters in one or jack of all trades?"

They aim to master everything they do,
Chasing perfection.
Like the jack of trades, they explore many skills,
But focus on one at a time, until they are close to mastery.

They want to be the greatest,
Not willing to settle for less.
With egos so vast, that they stretch like the cosmos,
Embracing the weight of their success.

Villains are thieves,
Cunning and mischievous.
They steal from geniuses,
From the greatest artists,
And from the highest achievers.
They steal their thought and ideas,
Not to seek praise,
But to fuel their ambitions
To perfect their craft and achieve mastery.

They makes mistakes quicker than most,
They are made fun of more than others.
Yet, they try new things, even without support.
So, they learn faster than others,
They achieve more,
They reach heights, higher than others

They don't chase what the world desires.
For them, money is just a tool.
Their goal isn't to be rich for the sake of proving
anything,
But to free themselves from the need for money.
But their true lifelong pursuit,
Is an endless journey of learning.
To keep growing,
To become the most capable—
Money, fame and all things superficial
Which ties the world
Can never hold them down.

Their opinions diverge from the norm.
The masses think, act, and follow the same patterns,
While they question everything.
Learning is their core focus,
Which marks them apart from the crowd.

They are masters of attachment and detachment,
Able to connect with anything or anyone,
And even get detached whenever they choose.
They constantly moving forward
Looking forward to new experiences and phases,
Flowing like water, never still.
Every moment is a new phase,
Every step, is a fresh adventure.

They don't judge others;
They have no time for gossip and judgment.
Their focus lies inward,
On their own journey,
Leaving no room for the noise of others.

Student: "What is learning? How does a villain learn?'
Master:
Villains are the gods of fascination
Fascinated by everything.
For them, even mistakes are valuable,
Even falling is acceptable—so long as they learn.
Their ultimate goal is learning.
They aren't bound by morality,
Or to portray themselves as noble.
They don't chase success, power or fame,
But if those come their way,
They use them as lessons, not trophies.
Always grounded in the pursuit of learning,
They lead their life,
Through ups and downs, always evolving.
That's what makes them so alive.
Humble and playful like a newborn kid,
They're constantly exploring.
Learning from everything and everyone.
They are not rigid thinkers,
Embracing even the most contradictory ideas,
Never clinging to a single belief.
Villains don't claim to know it all,
They remain forever fresh learners.
—

They are not corrupted.

Most people, once they reach success, fall victim to it.

But not villains—because for them, success is never the final goal.

They aren't swayed by the traps of power or fame;

They are driven by something deeper,

A relentless hunger to grow,

To learn, and to evolve.

Expect villains for whom success is not the final goal.

You can't corrupt villains.
They don't crave your money,
Or anything you offer.
Unlike heroes, they aren't driven by greed disguised as virtue.
They are self-sufficient,
Guided only by their sense of what is right,
What they truly want,
And what they genuinely desire.

"Master, Everyone believes in destiny, luck or the law
of attraction.
Do they work?" he asked.
The Master chuckled.
"If you let your destiny control you, you've already
lost," he said.
"It's like having a ship and letting it sail on its own,
Only to watch it sink.
You must take control of your destiny,
Learn to master the ship,
To master your fate.
Make your destiny your servant, my student,
The world is foolish for handing over the reins."

The boy, asks in awe—
"But master, how do I attain power?"

Self - mastery is the first step to true power.
To master your own emotions and thoughts,
Channeling them in ways that serve you.
When you master your inner world,
You unlock your potential and become unstoppable.

They master the dark arts—
Manipulation, power games, politics, war.
And they use it when necessary,
To accomplish the impossible,
To do what others deem unnecessary,
All for the greater good of the world.

The master gazes at the stars,
"Let me tell you about Kala, the master of dark arts,
Who became the most powerful king."

CHAPTER 5 - POWER

KALA, his age around age 50s

A king of one of the biggest kingdoms in the world,
His army is known as the greatest army ever,
And is feared far and wide.
The soldiers, unyielding warriors,
With mastery in martial arts, sword fights and archery

Every skill a warrior could possess.
The very name of the army strikes terror in the hearts
of kingdoms.
The intense echo of their march sends a shiver down
their spine.
Traumatising even the mightiest rulers.

The king, Kala, has eight generals and his guards,
Each one is equal to hundreds of warriors from other
kingdoms.
They are fiercely loyal,
Never leaving the king's side,
Always protecting him.

Kala is known to be the most powerful man.
Despite his power, he seeks freedom.
He prefers to fight alone,

For him, this world is like a playground,
He enjoys spending time with common people,
Sleeping in the house of a weaponsmith,
Touring other kingdoms in disguise as a simple
worker,
Making normal friends
Which is not liked by guards

He doesn't like to always have people around him.
He finds joy and fun in doing new things,
Trying out new experiences,
And enjoys his solo adventures.

But the guards, ever vigilant,
Want nothing more than to ensure his safety.
They see him as a cornerstone of the kingdom,
The one who manages everything,
They worry about him,
They cannot oppose the king,
For kala is arrogant and rude,
Often challenging them all at once.
But they always want to make sure he is safe no
doubt.

One day, A warrior— 8th feet tall,
Who is known as the greatest fighter,

With muscles as hard as iron,
He has fought uncountable battles and wars—
Challenges the king.

The guards, filled with pride
 Think they are enough to defeat him.
Just one guard attacks.
Only to get injured.
Then, two more join in,
But they too are harmed.

And then the king himself enters,
With just four moves,
In perfect synchronization of speed and strength,
Kala strikes the vital points.
And before anyone would notice what happened,
And even the mighty warrior could understand,
He was down.

All of them understood the true power of the king
that day.
Kala is capable of destroying kingdoms and building
them alone,
He alone can go into a kingdom
With strategy and manipulation,
He can create civil wars,

Or obliterate an entire realm,

Once, he went alone to a kingdom of evil.
They had captured and tortured a simple potter,
A common man.
Kala entered their land with burning eyes,
And returned alone,
Walking out of the fire and ashes of the fallen
kingdom.
And each step of his struck fear in those who
watched,
As if they were gazing upon the god of hell.
His eyes filled with rage,
This story made other kings fear just by hearing his
name.

But kala is a creator.
He built his kingdom from the ground up,
He is the one who taught his army skills they needed,
Mentored his generals in the art of war, manipulation,
strategy, martial arts, administration,
And even wealth creation.
He knows everything—
From weaponsmithing to pottery,
Every task that keeps the kingdom running.

His army reveres him,
Not just as a king,
But as their teacher.
They understand his true capabilities,
For he gives them their strength and power.

Despite being rude and arrogant,
Kala has a bond with his personal guards.
They all have fun like friends
Go out,
Drink and party,
Kala treats their family as his own,
Even the newest army recruit is family to him.
He always help them when needed,
Laughs and enjoys life alongside them.

One evening, as the guards were drinking and sharing
stories,
They asked the king,
"How did you become so powerful?" How are you
capable of so much?"
The king chuckled and replied
"When I was young, around 20s,
I was very weak.
I never had the courage to say 'no',
I used to always say 'yes',

Doing whatever anyone asked me.

I used to live in a city with my wife,
And my bosses, their men—
They would ask things of me,
And I used to comply.
And even if they teased me,
I wouldn't respond back.
I was naive and innocent
Thinking if I didn't fight back,

I will be safe,
I would survive.

But they never stopped taking advantage of me.
I was powerless and never went against,
Just to be safe.

And one day
They killed my wife.
And I lost everything I had—my family, my
happiness.

I was angry, but didn't know what to do.
I cried for help.
That's when I understood—

If you don't fight back,
 you will always be taken advantage of.
if I am not powerful,
Then people will keep harming and using me.
If I don't fight back,
If I don't have power
I will never be safe nor will be my family,

That's when I decided,
That night,
That moment ,
Under the dark sky with moonlight
I swore to become the most powerful man,
So powerful that no one could harm me again.
So powerful that I could protect anyone I cared about.
So powerful that even the gods couldn't suppress me.

I vowed on my wife's memory,
That from that moment on,
I will never be powerless again.
I would create the safest place for my people,
A place where no one would dare harm my family or my team.
Even if I have to become the *god of hell.*"

And That's when I met my master.
He is the one who taught me the reality of the world,
The dark arts, manipulation, art of war,
He is the one who helped me become this powerful."

The guards, furious at hearing this story,
Wanted revenge for their king.
Kala smiled and said,
"And I made sure my boss and his men experienced hell
For every breath they took."
And now here I am,
The guards smiled.

Months later, while the king was away from the kingdom,
Enjoying a serene lake alone,
A place his wife had loved,
He was ambushed at night
Many men attacked him all at once.
He barely survived a fatal blow,
But managed to escape,
Badly injured.

When he came back, his guards were furious,
One of his friends shouted at him.

And the king with his usual arrogance, shouted back,
"You are not able to find who is responsible and you
are shouting at me?
If you guys can't do it, leave me free!
I will take care of this in an hour."

And everyone knew he truly could handle it on his
own,
But his guards found the culprit and finished them.
The love-hate relationship between the king and his
guards,
Always brought a smile to his face.

The desire to have power is not wrong.

It's essential.

Without power, the world will suppress you.

But seek power not to dominate others,

But to ensure you're never dominated.

Become powerful

Not to control,

But to stay free.

Be the villain, if that's what it takes to rise.

If you are naive, be prepared to get hurt.
This world belongs to the fittest;
Only the strongest survive.
Like wild beasts, the world will devour you,
If you don't know your strengths.

A villain was once exploited—
Not for his wickedness, but for his kindness and naiveness.
He did good for everyone, always helpful,
But the world used him, took advantage of his heart.
He was kind, but blind to his power.
Until one day, he saw it.
He became the villain,
Not evil, just no longer a fool.

Still good, but now wise.
Strong enough to say no,
Realised his own strength,
Not to exploit others,
But to understand his worth,
And finally be free.

A villain is a master of self defense,
An expert in the art of war.
Cunning and unashamed,
They craft intricate plans,
Even when their reputation is on the line,
They know when to retreat,
Using that time to strategize.
Even if he has to run away,
His long term cunning art of war defeats the powerful
attacks.

They master the dark arts—
Manipulation, power games, politics, war.
And they use it when necessary,
To accomplish the impossible,
To do what others deem unnecessary,
All for the greater good of the world.

To defeat evil, one must become a greater evil.
Villains understand evil—they recognise it in others,
They know the thoughts most fear to explore,
As they never judged or restricted themselves with molarity,
They see through even the so-called heroes,
Because they embraced what others refused to face.
This is how they prevail.
They are the darkest of all,
Deep and dark as an endless pit—
Yet for the world, they shine as brightly as the sun.

Student:Master, but isn't it bad to learn manipulation
and things like that? Doesn't it make us bad people?
Master laughs,
"Learning the dark arts isn't about becoming bad,
It teaches you to see through deception,
To be careful from being preyed upon.
To use it when necessary—
Not for selfish gain, but for the greater good.
Never stop learning, learn everything there is,
Without judgment.
For example, when seeking something from others,
Knowing how to appeal to their desires,
Whether through charm or flattery, is a skill
In the world of politics,
Playing the game of power is essential for survival.

Life is a game, not of good or bad—
If you don't know how to play,
You will always fear it.
To be fearless, to be strong, to be powerful,
You have to understand the game,
And learn everything it takes to win.

If all you do is complain and cry, this world is cruel enough to overlook you.
Not to showcase your morality,
But to truly evolve and thrive.

If you don't know how to hunt,
You will always be afraid of the hunter.
If you don't know how to gain power,
You will always be afraid of the powerful.

Life is a game, not of good or bad—
If you don't know how to play,
You will always fear it.
To be fearless, to be strong, to be powerful,
You have to understand the game,
And learn everything it takes to win.

Everything fuels a villain's motivation—
Jealousy, insults, failure and even success.
No matter what life throws at them,
They turn it into energy to push forward.
For them, every experience is a spark to grow stronger.

Student: "Master in my life, there are people who want to disturb my peace."
Even when I ignore them, they keep coming.
They abuse me, torture me
Gather in crowds to hurt, bully and insult me.
What should I do, Master?
Should I keep ignoring them or fight back?

Master: "Don't ignore them. If you do, They'll mistake it for weakness and keep pushing.
Ignoring wrong doesn't make you strong—It makes you vulnerable,
You must fight back, but not blindly. Fight with strategy,
Using the art of war and power games.
Their goal is to provoke you,
If they come in gang,
You create your own gang.
Don't be foolish enough to be alone, don't be the hero, it only works in dramas.
Even the greatest villains need their gang,
What is a villain if they don't have a gang to support them.

You have to as powerful as possible—
Not to harm others,
But to not let anyone harm you.
And to support others when they are in pain
Power is the essential
And it should be the highest goal of every human
being—
To protect, to uplift, and to be unshakeable in the face
of adversity.

It's the law of the world:
The powerful survives.
If you are ignorant,
You will be prey for the hunters,
Vulnerable to those who seek to exploit your
weaknesses.
Gain power—
That kind that instills fear in every hunter,
The strength that commands respect.

If someone abuses you,
Hit them—not with just fists,
But with resolve and strength.
Don't let them win,
You are the villain in your own story.

"Master, I feel weak to say no,
 Sometimes I just say yes,
People use me and I can't do anything.
I am kind, but how do I stay strong? How do I say
no?" he asked.
"Learn to fight," The Master replied.
"Being stubborn in life is not wrong."
Fighting is not just about physical strength—
Saying no to someone who exploits you,
Choosing your path.
If you never fight your battles,
Never learn to say no,
And keep trying to please everyone,
You will never find your strength.
Fight for your right,
And make it a habit."

Student: master but the ultimate goal is peace, if you
read all the books or listen to gurus
Everything talks about love and peace
Master: peace, my ass
Peace comes from power
If you don't have power you can never be peaceful
Leave all those stupid books
The worlds reality is power dynamics
If you don't know them you will
Never be able to fulfill your ambition, your purpose
Nor will be able to gain power
And peace is very far
First be capable, then you think about peace

The boys says, Master Kala is so cool. He is truly amazing.

And he is thinking about Kala

The Master is about to leave and the boy asks

Wait,I want to know if there is any quality that he missed

That makes who villains are,

One new quality

The master says,

yes

CHAPTER 6 - INTELLIGENCE

Villains are intense with everything they do,
They want to live every second of their life with intensity.
They never let a moment pass idly.
Their time is precious, and they're adamant about spending it
With purpose, with passion.
They like to fulfill their ambitions with intensity.

They won't accept anything less than the thrill they
crave,
Their passion won't let them settle.
For them, pleasure, ambition and fun
They are not luxuries—they are necessities.
They are passionately focused on what they want,
Mad with purpose, refusing compromise.

They are very intense about the work they do
They are serious about their life, focused on their
goals.
They have seen life passing by,
They can't sit back without fulfilling what they set
out for.

Without intensity there is no meaning to life
They're intense creators and, equally, intense
destroyers.
They live for themselves to enjoy the lemons life has to
offer.
They are selfish about their own life,
Their own enjoyment.

They advance the society with their fierce desires and
their raw ambition,
Yet leave paths for destruction.

And among them, was Aaloka,
A villain as relentless and intense as a storm.
The boy, listening with wide eyes, asked,
"Who was Aaloka like? Why was he so... intense?"

The master chuckled,
"Aaloka... now, he was something else.
A man with a laugh that could rattle a room,
And a will so intense it was almost wild."

Story of Aalokha,

In a vast courtyard of a mighty kingdom,
A man is dancing in a wild manner.
Surrounded by bodies laid at his feet,
He was Aaloka, a name whispered in fear.

One of his guards approached with a crown,
Adorned with diamond, grand and bright.
Aaloka seized it, entranced by its gleam,
Eyes alight with his lust for wealth.

He craved all the luxuries life could grant,
An existence dripping in riches and vice.
Each moment a new indulgence,
An endless chase for the thrill.

Known as the god of naughtiness,
The god of trickery, feared and adored,
He owned no fortress of steel or stone —
But his true strength lies in his words.

With charm, deceit, and effortless lies,
He wove tales to twist and control.
Once the son of a mighty king,

A ruler now lost to time's shadow.

He bathes in the wealth,
 And follows his heart,
Which guides all his mischief.

He himself has no power but,
He gave people the comforts they desired,
Fed fears to bind them close,
He makes everyone thinks he is the most powerful,
Ruling their minds with crafted words.

The world he thought, is filled with fools.
He laughs when he fools others,
He charms his public,
By what they want to hear.
Making a way through their hearts.

He has the ability to fool anyone he likes
And always enjoys his way of doing things

He is the greatest con artist,
He cons the kingdoms into thinking he was power.
He either controls people, by desire or their fears.

His words are his superpower.

He hurts people using their weak points,
Cause them pain and mentally damages them.

He dreams of one day conning every being,
Of ruling every kingdom under his thumb.

One day, a strangers arrived in his court,
A master, intriguing, calm and shrewd.
Aaloka grinned, his curiosity stirred,
He invited the master into a game of wits.
They played the games of mind and skill—chess.
But Aaloka, to his shock, was defeated.
He asked the master, "Who are you?"
The master smiled, "Come with me and see."

The master spoke of three kingdoms at war,
A battle that threatened to consume the land,
The world itself could fall to ruin —
"Could be an interesting challenge for you."

Aaloka laughs hard and says,
"Why would I bother, what happens to the world or
you?
I have my kingdom bud."

The master says,

"Most importantly there are diamonds and a lot of
beauties
In those kingdoms."

Aaloka's eyes gleamed at the prospect of diamonds,
At the idea of beauties and spoils of war.
"Now that is worth fighting for, let's go,"
Leaving his guard, he followed alone.

They walked through deserts, barren and vast,
And with each step, a strange bond grew
Aaloka marveled at his companion's strength,
Saw how strong he was.

Aaloka realizes soon,
The master is not depending on him,
In Fact he needs no one, looking at how he
performed.
He asks, "Why bring me along?
You could have handled this on your own."

The master yawns, and calmly replied,
I was feeling lazy.
And I need a little entertainment .

Aaloka laughed,

"The world is full of fools,
But I feel challenged when I am with you,
It's a feeling I've never felt."

Master chuckled,
Glad to hear you're enjoying it.
Let's move now, the kingdom lies just beyond."

And they reach a kingdom,
Aaloka laid his traps,
Crafted lies, betrayals, and tricks,
Playing with the weakness of a noble man who never lied,
Or playing to the weakness of a decent man to protect his image.
He blackmails, hurts and plays mind games.

All three kings— deceivers, liars, schemers.
He read their soul like an open book,
And instead of war, he turned them to friends,
A union of power in a cunning alliance.

As they both start walking back on the desert,
Aaloka laughed, "You chose the wrong man
Now these kings are strong allies—
You'll never defeat them, master."

The master yawns once more, unbothered,
Together or apart, it matters not
For now let's return. That's another tale."
Aaloka scoffed, "I have outplayed you, friend."

Yet as they were walking, an army appeared,
An enemy harboring grudges deep
Aaloka sneered, "Seems like we're dead, bud."
And sat on the sand, ready to watch.
"Let's just get tortured and observe our own death
It should be interesting."

The master says,
"Don't worry I too will get it done soon."
And charged alone at the opposing force,
Weaponless yet fierce as thunder,
Turning their blades against them all.

In shock, Aaloka watched in awe,
As the master fought like a storm unleashed,
Until every foe lay vanquished, silent,
And the desert stretched quiet once more.

Aaloka, humbled, carried the master back,
Silently musing, pride now softened.
Upon their return, the master left,

But Aaloka waved him off with warmth.
He says, "I had the most fun doing this mission,"
The master smiled and left.

But even now, Aaloka didn't change,
Still driven by lust for luxury and sin.
He remains the god of mischief,
Dreaming to one day con the world.

Though he saved the world,
He still schemes against it.
A force needed for balance, they say.
For intelligence, be it dark or light,
Is a path the world must follow to grow.

Good or bad, it shapes the world,
Guided by curiosity's fire.
Aaloka was not the most intelligent,
But in the master he saw the glimpse of real strength.

Chapter 7 - Sharing

It's been quite some time since the master and the boy
had met.
Their bond grew deeper and stronger.
The boy full of curiosity and excitement, went to the
master and said,
"Master, can we go fishing?"
The master replied,
"Fishing, you say? Well, we could use a bit of a
break."

The Master and student went to the sea for fishing.
They cast their lines, and soon the student got lucky,
catching fish after fish,
While the master caught none.
The student filled with pride,
Proudly showed his catch to the Master,
And ventured farther into the sea to catch more.
Suddenly, a huge wave came, sweeping the student
away.
Panicked, he cried out—not knowing how to swim.
The master runs to save him,
Pulling him back to shore.
Once safe, the Master says,
You might be more capable than me,
In catching the fish,

But when it comes to swimming, I excel.
Never underestimate anyone.
You might be capable of fighting,
But your opponent might be capable of running and fleeing
If you ever underestimate anyone
You've lost the battle before it begins.
Always assess everyone's capabilities carefully,
And in doing so, you'll be humbled."

The boy laughed, so did the master.
They set a small fire nearby, warming themselves as they dried off,
Surrounded by the calming quiet of the evening.
The sky held the last, gentle rays of the setting sun, casting a warm golden glow.
The boy looked thoughtful, staring into the flames.
Finally he broke the silence.

"What is your purpose, Master?"

"To bring change," he said.

"To reshape the world and make it better.

To create an impact which will be remembered for generations."

Villains are the true teachers.
They don't expect anything from anyone;
They share their wisdom simply because they love to
teach.
They don't ask for anything in return,
Nor do they need anything in return,
Their strength comes from within,
Making them whole and complete.
In their lessons, we find power to grow,
Understanding that sharing knowledge is a gift of its
own.

They know the pain well,
They try not to let the pain get to others at once,
Yet, they don't stop it entirely.
They want to distance themselves, hoping to stay strangers,
But each time someone is experiencing pain,
They feel the pain too.

Not able to see other's pain
They pray that
All the pain in the world
Should be carried by them
And that's how they became the strongest

The more intense the love is,
The greater the heartbreak.
And the villains, with their fierce intensity,
Are the ones who love the hardest,
And break the most.

They started their journey to change the world,

To do things for the welfare of the world.

Their mission was clear:

To improve and develop the world beyond its current

state.

Villains choose their mentors carefully,
Taking time to investigate and reflect.
Once they find the right guide,
They commit to the journey,
Unlearning new habits and embracing new lessons.
They become open to learn everything,
And after their apprenticeship,
They become students of the greatest mentor, Life.
Continuously learning, adapting, and evolving.
With humility, They submit to teachings.
Always, questioning and seeking deeper
understanding.
This way, they become life's most dedicated learners.

They obey their duties,
Born from a deep love.
Even if they have to be unfair,
Or appearing weak to the world,
They always choose love.
The villain hugs his enemies,
Helping them rediscover who they once were,
Transforming foes into friends,
Showing that strength can be gentle,
And love can heal even the deepest wounds.

The scars of the battle mean little to them,
But the scars of the people who betrayed them cut
deep.
They wear a smile and move on
Each betrayal forging their resolve,
Building walls around their hearts.
But beneath the tough exterior,
They remain the world's greatest lovers.
No room for vengeance, even against those who have
wronged them,
For their hearts are filled with understanding and
love.

They share quietly,
No one sees their kindness,
For the world labels them as villains,
Yet deep down, they are lovers,
Caring in ways unseen.

"Master, were you always this strong?" he asked.

The Master laughed, louder than ever.

"No, in fact, I was more foolish and naive than you are.

I was weaker, a people-pleaser and someone no one noticed.

But I decided to move on the path of learning, growing and achieving greatness.

This path was filled with hardships,

And those hardships that made me who I am today.

If you want to grow, take the path of achieving greatness.

Be the greatest there ever was, or will be.

Don't settle.

Keep learning,

Keep growing.

Even now, there is a lot for me to learn and grow student."

Their love is not a burden,
But it sets them free.
They don't need anyone by their side to feel it,
They simply love.
They don't ask for anything in return,
No promises, no conditions,
Their love remains.
They never cling or demand,
Everyone is free to leave
No one owes them anything for their love—
They just love.

They are masters of attachment and detachment,
Able to connect with anything or anyone,
And even get detached whenever they choose.
They constantly move forward
Looking forward to new experiences and phases,
Flowing like water, never still.
Every moment is a new phase,
Every step is a fresh adventure.

They do not grow weak from love;
They are strengthened by it.
They love everyone,
But that doesn't mean they turn a blind eye.
if someone attacks them, they attack back,
When evil rises, they confront it.
Even if they love those who stray,
They don't hesitate to challenge them,
To free them from their darkness.
Their actions stem not from rage or hate,
But from a deep love for all,
A desire to uplift, to protect,
Believing in a better world for everyone.

The villain came from distant lands to build a life in the city.
He worked tirelessly, overcoming countless challenges,
And finally created something of his own.
But then, he decided to give it all away for his family,
Villain's friend: "You will lose everything you built till now."
Villain: When I first came here. Did I have anything?
I built it once, and I'll build it again—this time even faster."

People in this world don't have gratitude
And the villain never does anything for gratitude
They neither expect gratitude nor love
It's for their own satisfaction

They reinvent themselves as often as necessary,
Destroying their weaker selves.
To rise again, stronger and more resilient,
Each transformation is a rebirth,
A chance to shed the past
And embrace new strength.

Villains don't show love,
They simply love.
The ones who make a display of it,
Hold only the surface.
But the one who truly loves,
Keeps it hidden,
Silent.
Deep within.

CHAPTER 8 - LOVE

It was night time,
The master asks the boy,
"If you could meet any villain, who would it be?"

The boy gree curious
But had no answer,
Excitement filled his body,
Mind full of questions.

He thought of Kala,
Then Tamish,
But he says he is confused and would like to meet..
And got lost in thought.

Suddenly, a tap on his shoulder.
He turned around,
And there stood a huge man,
Draped in gold,
A royal outfit shimmering in the dark.

This man,
With an awe-inspiring physique,
And a face so handsome
The boy couldn't look away.

He knew instantly, who it was,
It was Kala.

Overwhelmed, he stood still.
Here was one he'd only heard of,
Thought so much of,
Right before him.

Kala smiled,
And greeted him,
The boy froze in shock.

Turning to the master,
Kala asked,
"What brings you to the forest, master?"
And they embraced,
While the boy stood mesmerized.

Master looks at Kala,
And says, "You have grown a lot.
It's been so long."

Kala laughed,
"Let's talk over some food.
Why did you call me to a forest?
I'm starving!

I'll be back in 10 minutes."

Kala strode into forest,
And hunted a huge animal,
And carried it back on his back.

As Kala walked back to their camp,
The boy heard footsteps,
Turned to see Tamish and Kshipa,
Walking towards them.

Excited, he smiled—
More villains were joining them.
Tamish and Kshipa came closer
And exchanged hugs with the master.

Tamish, young and vibrant,
With a lean muscular, frame
And a shiny smile.
Kshipa looked like the most beautiful girl,
With elegance all over her.
She moves swiftly with elegance,
Talked smoothly, with a sweet voice,
Had the warmest smile of all .

Kala gestured towards the food,

"Look, this meal will be incredible."
Tamish grinned,
"Wow, Can't be better.
Let's tear it up, and feed.
I am starving from all the walking."

Kshipa glanced around,
"Where are the others?
 It's nearly dawn."
Tamish rolled his eyes,
Don't ask.
They're the closest, yet they'll still be last."

Kshipa is bothered by some small bug roaming
around them,
When suddenly,
An arrow flew through the air,
Striking it down,
The master catching it mid-air,
And consuming it.
From the shadows,
Dhana appeared,
His bow resting on his shoulder,
Walking with a precise, quiet confidence.

The boy, amazed by his precision,

In the night with only few fire sticks,
Couldn't take his eyes off him.

He came close to everyone, and greeted each.
And all of them made a fireplace and sat beside
And began to eat.

From the trees above,
A sound came.
Tamish, Kshipa, and the boy grew alert,
But the others simply ate.

With a grand entrance,
Someone from above the trees jumped,
And it's Aloka with his naughty entry.
Still the Master, Kala and Dhana didn't flinch.

Aaloka grinned,
"Come on, you know my entrance was impressive!"

Kala smirked,
"Eat fast, or you'll miss the meal."

Aaloka, with his luxurious clothes,
Diamond-studded necklace,
And shining hair under the moonlight,

Sat next to the boy.

After the meal,
The boy asked Kala if he could ask questions.
They walked to the riverbank,
Moonlight glimmering on the water,
And finally, his questions spilled out.

The boy couldn't stop his questions
One question, above all,
He had to know—
The story of the master.

And kala, having no choice, began.

Story of the Master:

"Our master,
A child of ambition,
Who dreamed of power,
Of peace,
And of ruling one day.

He was born in a unknown village,
As a weak, fragile kid,
He didn't have the strength like others,

And was mocked.

Yet he was determined,
To love everyone,
To help everyone,
To change the world and make it better.

He wanted to become a hero,
And save the world.
As a kid, he helped everyone,
Even though he was going through his own problems.
He never stopped showing love to people
Even to those who didn't love him.

Stronger he became,
And harder grew his challenges,
But as he helped others,
He grew stronger.

When he grew up,
He fell in love,
He wanted to be around her.
Be for her,
And when she fell in danger,
He met his heroes,
Only to find his heroes,

Were monsters behind masks.

His world shattered.
He saw the truth—
Evil cannot be defeated,
By mere goodness.

So, for her,
He chose to become a demon,
Burn down the world, to light up his own.

So the journey to become the greatest evil started,
South he traveled,
To an island of outcasts,
Gangsters, thieves and demons,
Where he found no mercy.

His ambition had changed into becoming,
The most ruthless, heartless, demon.

He went to those lands to conquer it,
He helped the other demons and freed them.

Yet none of the people in the kingdom wanted him as
king.

Everyone had their ego and wanted to be king
themselves.

But the master showed them who had true power.
One by one,
He fought them all,
Showed them, his strength,
Cutting down anyone who defied him.

Anyone who were to not obey him, would be
punished,
They swore loyalty,
And he built a kingdom,
Of thieves, warriors and rogues.

The outside world wanted his downfall,
Attacked for years,
Yet he protected his kingdom,
Leading them through famine and suffering.

In time, the world gave up,
And he truly became *the Demon King*.

He then went on wars and destruction for resources,
He build one of the greatest kingdoms,
With prosperity for everyone.

His kingdom was feared by all,
His name was feared and echoed throughout.
He tamed monsters had his personal guards,
One blow from him and the world would be in
shackles.

But in his heart,
He still felt alone.
She never returned,
His world.

He took a student and taught him,
Who later betrayed him.
Everyone he loved,
Left him behind.
He had fear, respect throughout his kingdom
But love was what he craved.

To save someone was what made him powerful,
To share with someone was what made him strong.
To teach someone was what made him so great.

Yet, he still was a great king.

But unfortunately, the world conspired against him
again.
He lost his kingdom, he lost all the people in his
kingdom
He barely managed to get saved,
As he saw.
His island was turned into ashes of hell.

He kept walking alone in the desert.
No one knows what happened after,
Yet his childhood dream never ended,
His ambitions are still alive,
He is still the same child who loves everyone,
Who shares whatever he has.
And he is still the ruthless demon.
Who everyone fears.

He feels warm to be around all,
But sometimes you can feel the darkness around him,
Like a void pulling you in.

I still don't understand him.
No one does.
He roams, full of mysteries, wanting to be unfolded,
By someone who knew and loved him,

The boy, calm now,
Listened, as the river flowed,
Moonlight dancing on the water.
"Are there not seven villains?"
I've only heard of five." he asked.
Kala replied,
"Two are dead—
They both are dead,
One is known as the king of the seas,
The other, the blind archer,
More powerful than all of us combined,
Their bond with our master was legendary,
Achieving what few could dream."

The boy whispered,
" I wish to know their story."
Kala smiled,
"You will one day, when the time is right."

Then Kala asked,
"Now, tell me, how did you meet the master?

The boy blushed,
Recounting his own story,
And Kala smiled.

"You have a long journey ahead of you," said Kala
"I hope life gives you trials,
So you may become stronger than us all."

The boy protested,
"No, I don't think I will become as strong as you
people."

Kala chuckled,
"Master never chooses wrongly,
And you, with your questions,
Have great potential.
Few know as much as you do,
Or care to learn."

The boy smiled,

Kala said,
"Lets sleep,
It seems tomorrow will be a long day."

As they woke,
The villains turned to the master,
"Is there a mission?" they asked.

And the master replied,

I want to conquer the kingdom where the boy came
from."

Kala laughed,
"You called me for this?
My assistant's assistant could have handled it."

Tamish scoffed,
"If you'd told me last night,
It would have already been done."

Kshipa, in jest,
"Master, shall i go announce the war?"

Dhana chucked,
"Is this child's play for us?
That young boy looks enough."

The boy, wide- eyed, whispered,
"Me?"
Aloka chimed in,
"Sounds fun, let's make it grand."

And with that,
They set off towards the kingdom,
The boy, one of them now.

The master handed him his horse,
And they rode out,
A new journey ahead.

FINAL NOTE

Thank you for taking the time to read *Be the Villain*. I hope this book has inspired and empowered you to embrace your unique journey, confront challenges with courage, and seek authenticity in all aspects of life. Remember, every setback is an opportunity for growth, and the true villains are those who remain true to themselves.

May your life be filled with challenges, opportunities to grow, and find the strength to be the villain in your own story, rewriting the narrative to reflect your true self.

Follow me on social media to get more interesting content about Villains

Instagram: www.instagram.com/thelaziestpoet/
LinkedIn: www.linkedin.com/in/yaseenahmadsk/

Thank you for your support!